The Power of the Sun

is concentrated in every part of growing plants—and passed on to us when we eat them in their natural states. Yet by cooking, milling, and refining, we destroy much or all of their value, and at the same time add to our diets such foods as meat which both displace needed fruits and vegetables and add their own poisons to our systems.

Watching patient after patient gain nearly instant relief from long-lasting disease by following his regimen convinced Dr. Bircher-Benner of the immense curative power of natural foods—a discovery you can repeat for yourself with this book.

the Bircher-Benner
Raw Fruits & Vegetables Book

Max E. Bircher, M.D. &
M. Bircher-Benner, M.D.

Revised Translation with Foreword by
REGINALD SNELL

NUTRITION CENTERS, INC.
1315 Memorial Dr. Asbury Park, N.J.
988-2020

650-D Newman Springs Rd. Lincroft, N.J.
741-2929

139 Brighton Ave. West End, N.J.
229-6636

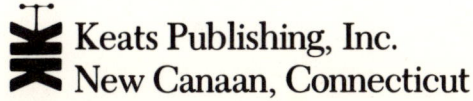
Keats Publishing, Inc.
New Canaan, Connecticut

RAW FRUITS & VEGETABLES BOOK

Published in 1977 by Keats Publishing, Inc.
By arrangement with the C.W. Daniel Company, Ltd.
London, England

Copyright© 1946 by Drs. Max E. Bircher and M. Bircher-Benner
Special contents copyright© 1977
by Keats Publishing, Inc.

All rights reserved

Library of Congress Catalog Card Number: 77-723-88

Printed in the United States of America

Keats Publishing, Inc.
36 Grove Street, New Canaan, Connecticut

Contents

FOREWORD vii

PREFACE ix

Chapter

I INTRODUCTORY 1
II THE PREPARATION OF UNCOOKED FOOD 6
III FOODSTUFFS 11
IV RECIPES OF UNCOOKED DISHES 16
    (a) Raw Fruit Porridge 16
    (b) Cold Fruit Dishes (Macédoine) 25
    (c) Fruit Juice Mixtures and Nut Milk 26
    (d) Raw Vegetables 28
    (e) Raw Food Dishes (Hors d'oeuvres) 30
    (f) Raw Vegetable Juices 37
    (g) Exclusive Raw Food Day 39
    (h) Menus for Raw Food Meals 40
V EXAMPLES OF DIET DAYS 44
    1. Normal Day 45
    2. Transitional Day 49
    3. Raw Food with a Supplementary Dish ... 52
    4. Strict Raw Food Days 53
    5. Fruit Fasting Days 56

Foreword

SINCE the last (revised and enlarged) edition of this book was published in the year of Dr. Bircher-Benner's death, a good deal of nutritional history has been made. During six years of food emergency we have been carrying out—however unwillingly in some cases—much that he recommended, at least in a negative sense; and in spite of (or as believers in his teaching would say, at least in part because of) the severe cut in animal protein foods, the shortage of sugar, and the scarcity of sweet cakes made from finely-milled flour, we find the general standard of national health notably improved.

The present revision of this important guide to the new nutritional teaching has involved some hundreds of alterations. Some of them are matters of detail, but most are concerned with bringing the terminology employed into line with the accepted usage of the youngest of the sciences, and with helping the housewife in the practical carrying out of Bircher-Benner's instructions, some of which are apt to sound more difficult than they really are.

A number of practical directions suggested by wartime conditions, and for particular use in this country, have been incorporated (in footnotes, signed with her initials) by the distinguished food therapist, Mrs. Claire Loewenfeld, pupil of Dr. Bircher-Benner and holder of a special teaching diploma at his Zürich clinic. I am most grateful to her for this valuable help. For other signed footnotes, as for the entire revision of the previous translation, I am responsible. The author's own footnotes are unsigned.

REGINALD SNELL

St. Christopher School, Letchworth.

Preface

THE first thing we have to do is to recognize facts and the second to apply them. On this application depends our whole life from beginning to end.

This booklet has been written with the purpose of putting into practice our new knowledge regarding nutrition. But this knowledge is new only to the scientific world; it has been the precious possession of mankind from time immemorial. Putting it into practice does not, therefore, mean introducing a new kind of food, but the food destined to be man's by the wisdom of the Creator. Raw food has, in fact, been known for thousands of years in China and India; it is also mentioned in the Bible.

Nutrition is not the highest thing in life, but it is the soil on which the highest things can either perish or flourish. Erroneous dietetics or ignorance and comtempt of the true laws of nutrition have done incalculable harm to mankind. Many see the harm, for illnesses appear sooner or later, but only a few know the real cause of them: wrong food. Illusion and error which so often rule men and mislead them, make us believe in connections and causes which on closer examination prove to be insignificant and secondary. We speak of chills and bacteria when we should say wrong nutrition. The harm created can only be prevented or—where it is not too late—remedied by attacking the real cause.

The following important facts should be noticed in connection with this new knowledge:

I. The quantity of protein hitherto said to be necessary was far too high. The human organism requires a minimum quantity of protein (not more than 7 percent of the calories necessary). The daily excess of protein overtaxes the vital organs and produces chronic acidity of the tissues and juices.

II. The most extravagant and poorest kind of food is certainly meat, whether butcher's meat, game, poultry or fish. It causes the greatest loss of energy in the metabolic combustion, too much acidity in the chemical proportions and, moreover, poisons the organs, the tissues and the blood with uric acid.

III. Eggs and cheese, among other animal food, cause over-acidity, and milk often loses its value through cooking and becomes even dangerous through the wrong feeding of the cows or the widespread disease of their udders.

IV. The three chief nutritive elements hitherto known were protein, carbohydrates and fat. By themselves they cannot nourish the body. A mysterious "Something" is needed which is found in the vegetable kingdom, built up by the power of the sun and called "Vitamins." This something is found in perfect quality and in sufficient, often abundant, quantity in fresh fruit, berries, vegetable fruits (tomatoes, cucumbers), in green leaves (spinach, cabbage, salad leaves and herbs), and in those roots which can be eaten raw (carrots, celery, onions, etc.). The milk which the cows produce when they have been fed on green grass during the months of May, June, July and August also contains vitamins, and so does the butter made from that milk. Among animal foods, few of the organs in their raw state contain sufficient vitamins, and these are lost through cooking, roasting, sterilizing and pasteurizing. This is equally the case when dried food is exposed to the air. The vitamins of cereals (rice, wheat, maize, etc.) disappear when subjected to the usual grinding process, owing to the elimination of the germ. White bread lacks vitamins.

V. Total lack of vitamins is the exception, but may occur when old-fashioned dietetic prescriptions are ordered. In this case serious diseases occur after six or eight months, such as general inflammation of the nerves, and scurvy. Partial lack of vitamins produces at first slight derangements of health, such as digestive troubles, constipation, functional disturbances of the heart and blood circulation; it prevents the growth of the body and causes goiters, etc. After many years serious diseases occur, amongst which cancer is the most terrible.

VI. The nutritive habits of civilized people (e.g. hotel cooking) have taken us out of the true way of living, for we have preferred animal food, white bread, preserves, cooked and roasted food. We have overtaxed our blood with excessive acidity and an accumulation of uric acid and in this way originated an immense number of chronic diseases. The causal connections remain wholly in the dark, so that hardly anyone discovers the reason of his suffering to be wrong food.

VII. The secret of vitamins, which cannot be reduced to chemical-material elements, is to be explained in terms of energy. It was a thoughtless mistake to suppose that the living cell could feed on calories. It is only sustained by the electromagnetic energies of the sunlight which are stored up in the vegetable kingdom and provide us with our food. The nutritive energy of a cherry, an orange, a green leaf, is stored sunlight, composed of the richly coloured scale of vibrations of the rainbow (sunspectrum). But the vibrations of the light which is contained in the substance, will be lost through heating; they equally disappear when the germ, which is charged with fine mineral-containing molecules, is eliminated from the corn. Our food may contain proteins, carbohydrates and fats in the richest profusion, and nevertheless have completely lost the sunlight. It contains, indeed, more than enough calories, but its light is dull and smouldering. Such food gives insufficient nourishment and is apt to produce illness. Sunlight food keeps us healthy and strong and has power to correct the diseases caused by other foods. Nowadays with our knowledge of the construction of atoms, of the absorption and emission of light rays through the orbits of the electrons, it should be easy for any scientific mind to understand the importance of the sun quality of our food. But the ramshackle structure of the old nutritional teaching, in which we have been so comfortably resting, would collapse, and with it a great deal of which routine has accustomed us. We should have to acknowledge our mistakes, think out and learn new ways. Far too uncomfortable a thing! And yet what really nourishes the body is the energy of the sun which is stored up in the formation of vegetable food-stuffs (that is, the vitamins), not mere heat.

VIII. Deficiency of vitamins and of alkaline-forming foods, excess of acid-forming foods, lack of sunlight—all these are really one and the same thing—such are in fact the chief causes of the most serious and widespread diseases to which mankind is subject.

IX. All these diverse, protracted and serious illnesses can be prevented by sunlight food.

X. The decision to part with the old ways and to adopt the sunlight foods opens to mankind a new way to spiritual possibilities, and also to therapeutic measures in the physical sphere. In any case the sunlight food is, amongst all remedies that are not of a spiritual nature, the most important one. The curative power of this food is in inverse proportion to the power of the customary diet of civilized Europeans to promote disease among the misguided and unsuspecting people who accept it.

So much for the new knowledge.* Now comes the question, how are we to apply it? What is our food to consist of? This booklet has been written with a view of answering the question.

Many changes can be introduced to our daily meals: the quantity of meat can be reduced, or meat can be omitted altogether. Instead of white bread we can eat wholemeal bread (the best is made of wheat and rye). We can feed chiefly on cooked vegetarian diet (vegetables, farinaceous food, rice, potatoes, etc.). To this can be added raw fruits of all kinds, nuts, roots and salads. The use of alcoholic drinks, coffee, tea, chocolate, cocoa, can be omitted or reduced. This is a step in the right direction, but the *curative* power of such a dietary change is small.

In connection with this it may be mentioned that a lady patient had been consulting a doctor who was a great authority, and had been recommended by him to give up meat. She did so, but grew weaker and weaker. Why was this the case? Because her vegetarian diet consisted of vegetables, the boiling of which had deprived them of all nutritive value; also of fine flour dishes, eggs, rich milk, cheese and butter which neither contained enough vitamins and alkalis, nor was it rich enough in "sunlight" value. The lady now consulted another specialist who, indignant on hearing of

---

*For a fuller scientific explanation of this whole subject, see *Food Science for All—A New Sunlight Theory of Nutrition* by Dr. Bircher-Benner, translated and edited by Arnold Eiloart, B. Sc., Ph.D.

the treatment recommended before, said that a meatless diet was nonsense and that she was at once to begin with "nourishing" food, especially meat. This also was carried out, but the illness grew rapidly worse. A third doctor abroad was consulted, who advised her to give up meat, and to begin the diet which is put forth in this booklet. This she did, and after six months she came to Zürich, paid me a visit and told me how grateful she was for the advice of my booklet, which she had followed carefully. A considerable improvement of her conditions had already taken place.

When we have to get rid of an illness, a greater effort is necessary on the part of the patient than if we have only to maintain health. Lack of vitamins has exhausted the tissues and organs. The surplus acidity can only be got rid of gradually. Because of the accumulation of the poisons of metabolism the body needs a long time for the diet to take its effect, so that their elimination can begin. A crisis has to take place sooner or later before any improvement is generally noticed. And everyone who has eaten the customary diet over a period of years, even the apparently healthy person, has a poisonous metabolic condition in his tissues.

A firm resolution is therefore required on the part of the patient, at the outset of the therapeutic process. He has definitely to give up his old ways and begin with several days a week, perhaps even several weeks, of exclusively raw food. This has to consist of all sorts of fresh fruit, nuts (walnuts, hazelnuts, sweet almonds, pine kernels, etc.), the fruits, roots, stalks and leaves of vegetables and green herbs.

Experience has shown that in consequence of the weakness of our teeth and digestive organs, this raw food must be chopped to a large extent. A tasty combination must also be made, for by making it appetizing, one succeeds more easily in winning the patient over to the new diet, thus hastening the process of cure.

The booklet also contains menus made up of cooked and raw food combined. This mixed food may be eaten alternately with the raw food. The mixed but meatless diet can by itself show its curative power and also prevent illness. It contains abundant raw material, and what is cooked has been chosen and prepared with special care. Even those who are difficult to please can thus have a diet which will help them to keep good health all their lives.

The method of preparing the dishes, the getting-up of the menus, will be found in the cookery book entitled *Health-Giving Dishes* , compiled by B. Brupbacher-Bircher.

M. BIRCHER-BENNER, M.D.

Zürich, August 1936.

RAW FRUITS
& VEGETABLES
BOOK

I
Introductory

"Sunlight dishes" I should like to call the pure food which has not been denatured either by heat or extraction of certain properties in cooking. It is a source of real strength to the weak, an unpretentious and yet powerful remedy for the sick, the preserver of sound teeth, of capable digestive organs and of a clean, healthy-coloured complexion. Moreover, in it is found the fundamental force of resistance against all infection. Why should I like to call it "Sunlight Food"? You will find the answer to this question in the author's book on *A New Sunlight Theory of Nutrition*.* The name "Sunlight Food" touches the very heart of the matter.

Let us call it simply uncooked food; food that has not been denatured by the heat of the fire. Whatever nutritive principles the wisdom of nature has put into it are always found therein whole and entire. The substances which we take into our digestive organs in this food are still full of undestroyed vitality and not, like the substances of cooked food, deadened and destroyed by heat. That is why it has a different effect from cooked

*See page xiii footnote.

food. It nourishes better, it strengthens more, it increases health, revives the organs, purifies the blood, casts out poisons and bacteria from the body. It is a genuine reliable remedy. A well-known French medical man, a professor who had studied its curative effects in the treatment of the sick, called it "matière vivante"—living matter.

When it was usual to feed babies artificially with sterilized (long-boiled) milk, many of them became ill with scurvy and died suffering fearful pains, all because of the food received. It was then discovered that by feeding babies on the fresh juice of apples, oranges and carrots and on unboiled milk, they soon recovered. One might have made the same discovery with the fresh juice of raspberries, currants, bilberries, cherries or grapes. This proved, at least in the case of infants, that the heat of cooking can spoil food so much that it produces a deadly disease which only the "matière vivante," the "sunlight food," can cure. But also with older children and grown-up people a diet consisting exclusively or even predominantly of cooked denatured food has disastrous effects. Unfortunately these are often not easily recognized, as people attribute them to other causes and treat them with all kinds of strange remedies, instead of the only right one: uncooked food. A striking example of such effects is chronic constipation, one which is well known and which again can lead to a whole host of diseases such as auto-intoxication (self poisoning), appendicitis, diseases of the sexual organs, of the heart and blood vessels, the liver, the kidneys, etc. Constipation is a widespread evil and is treated with pills, herbal teas, irritating oils, mineral salts and waters, water, oil and glycerine enemas and all kinds of abdominal massage, until one finds in the end that all these remedies have

INTRODUCTORY

no longer any effect whatever. But few people take to the only true and reliable remedy, uncooked food. It is a matter for both shame and astonishment that people who suffer from chronic constipation, and obtain no help from any remedy, achieve again a regular action of the bowels, in a short time, with competent and experienced treatment by uncooked food. American doctors have also observed that the most obstinate constipation known as the "Hirschsprung disease," which begins even in infancy and against which no remedy was known, could be cured by feeding the patient exclusively on uncooked food.

But do not let us forget that constipation is only a simple instance of the noxious effect of the wrong diet, just as its cure is an example of food therapy by means of right feeding. The amount of harm done through wrong nutrition is enormous and can hardly be gauged; certainly not in this Introduction the aim of which is simply to give reasons for the value of uncooked food, and instructions for its preparation. Let it suffice to say that the value of uncooked food is doubly proved: first by the abundance and all-sufficiency of nourishing power which nature has put into it, and second by its restoring the health that man has squandered through ignorance and misunderstanding of nutrition.

But before describing the dishes and their preparation, let me say one more word about the reason which makes us *prepare* natural and fresh food instead of simply using it as it is. It is to be found in the actual state of civilized man's digestive organs and also in the fact that our stomachs have been spoilt by long habituation to cooked food. It is not necessary to explain that in the case of scorbutic infants one has to squeeze apples, oranges, etc., and to give them only the juice or grated pulp of the fruit. Grown-up people have often, however, either bad teeth or at least bad nutritive habits. The child follows their example as soon as possible; careful chewing and salivating of the food is no longer a universal habit. Nearly everybody gobbles. Eating in this way can, perhaps, be practised with cooked food—at least trouble does not follow immediately—but it is impossible with uncooked food. Weak digestive organs and flaccid intestines cannot properly assimilate and utilize such food as is not carefully broken up. Fermentation easily takes place in the bowels, digestive troubles begin, and thus the first timid attempts to make use of uncooked food usually come to nothing, particularly in the case of sufferers from stomach trouble. If people have already had unfortunate experiences from eating fresh fruit, cucumbers, etc., and have already been warned by medical men against uncooked food, then such digestive troubles are in their eyes a confirmation of all their doubts and other people's warnings. They are convinced, for their own experience has proved that stomach and bowels cannot stand raw food. This conviction, in spite of all plausible confirmations by experience, is an error that has serious consequences. Precisely those people who suffer from indigestion need this raw food, and the stomach stands it amazingly well, as soon as the food is properly prepared.

Then, too, the fact is that people are unfortunately accustomed to eating cooked food. The palate has become very exacting. The organs of taste demand stronger stimulants, the palate a softer touch than the pure, raw materials, for instance salad or cabbage leaves, are able to give. Our organs of taste are blunted and uncooked food seems insipid if we accustom our palate to the taste of roasted food, much addition of salt, mustard, pepper and other spices. This is all the more

INTRODUCTORY

the case when people live little in the open air, when apéritifs, wine and beer are taken with and before meals and when smoking is habitual. It is only when the habit of eating cooked food has been broken for some time that they begin to enjoy the far more varied and delicious taste of uncooked dishes.

II

The Preparation of Uncooked Food

The preparation of uncooked food ought to overcome all the above mentioned obstacles and difficulties as much as possible. There are various ways of preparation: squeezing, cutting or grating into small pieces, and mixing with various ingredients to make up a dish. But every preparation has to be preceded by a careful selection of the raw materials, cutting off the parts that are not absolutely fresh or that are indigestible, and carefully cleaning the rest.

A few technical indications and illustrations of the necessary implements are added:

Lettuce leaves, cress, corn-salad (lamb's lettuce), endive and the like are to be put for an hour into strongly salted water, then carefully washed under the tap or in water several times renewed.

Apples should be rubbed with a clean cloth and afterwards the calyx, the stalk, and any bad parts are cut out. Then they are cut in two, so as to be sure that there is no worm inside.

Roots like carrots, radishes (black and ordinary), kohlrabi, celeriac are carefully washed in running water and then scraped; the hard, woody parts should be cut off. Cut celeriac gets black when exposed to the air, and therefore must be put into water with a little lemon juice in it.

Cabbages should be cleaned like lettuces. The tender parts only must be used for dishes of uncooked food.

SOAKING BEFOREHAND

If, towards spring, fresh fruit is lacking, dried fruit must be resorted to: figs, prunes, apple rings, pears, apricots, sultanas, raisins, etc. Wash them first in hot water, then soak them in plenty of water for twenty-four hours. They absorb the water, get soft and are thus easily cut up. In that soaked state the stones of stone fruit are easily removed.

Cereal preparations such as rolled oats, rice-flakes, wheatflakes or groatflour are to be soaked for twelve hours in three times as much water as their own volume.

SQUEEZING

Cut oranges and lemons in two and press them out on the lemon squeezer. It is made of china, glass or enamel (see Illustrations 1 and 2).

Different kinds of berries are most easily pressed out in the juice extractor (see Illustration 3). One can thus get the purée or the juice of the berries, as desired. With the same extractor one can get the juice of fresh apples, pears, plums, apricots, etc., or the purée of dried fruit, soaked beforehand.

CUTTING AND GRATING

For this purpose use a knife or a grater of finer or

RAW FRUITS AND VEGETABLES BOOK

Illustration 1.—Orange and lemon squeezer made of glass

Illustration 2.—Economical lemon and orange squeezer

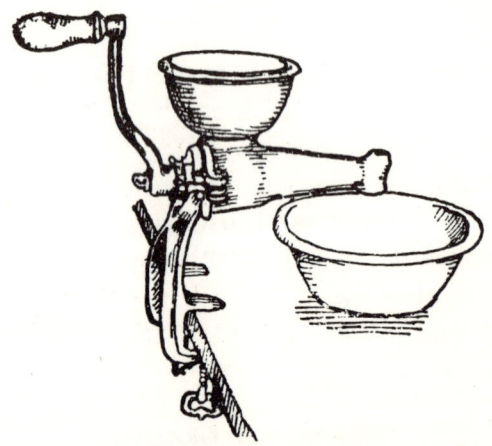

Illustration 3.—Juice extractor

THE PREPARATION OF UNCOOKED FOOD

coarser grain, or the mincing machine; for nuts and almonds the nutmill (see Illustrations 4, 5, 6 and 7).

Illustration 4.—Grater with three parts

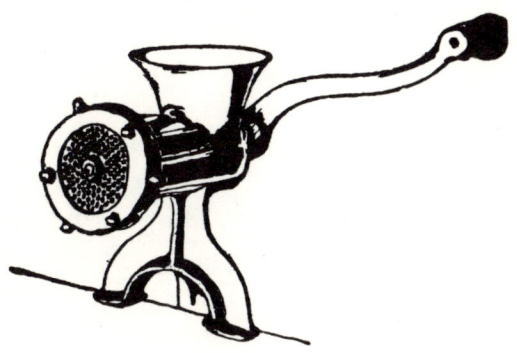

Illustration 5.—Mincer

Illustration 6.—Two-way grater ("Better-grip") for apples and raw food salads

RAW FRUITS AND VEGETABLES BOOK

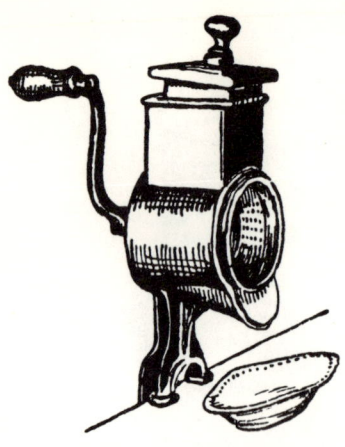

Illustration 7.—Mill for nuts and almonds

NOTICE ESPECIALLY

The preparation and mixing of uncooked food should only be done shortly before it is served. Such food must not be kept standing for hours after having been prepared.

III

Foodstuffs

It is taken for granted that the foodstuffs used for dishes of uncooked food are taken from the vegetable kingdom, with the exception of milk, milk products and eggs, which are only used in moderate quantities.*

Nature has provided us with a rich choice of suitable foodstuffs. Various different groups are here mentioned, with representatives of each.

1. *Fruits:* apples, pears, oranges, grapes, cherries, damsons, plums, apricots, greengages, peaches, bananas, pomegranates, dates, lemons, grapefruit, pineapples, figs, etc.

2. *Berries:* strawberries, raspberries, blackberries, red and black currants, bilberries, cranberries, gooseberries, etc.

3. *Vegetables:*
(a) (the fruit of the plant): cucumbers, pumpkins, melons, tomatoes, etc.

---

*The reason for this cannot be explained here. This question of nutritional teaching is treated in the author's book *Food Science for All* (see page xiii footnote).

(b) (the leaf of the plant): cabbage, lettuce, cos lettuce, endive, dandelion leaves, spinach, various cresses, corn-salad (lamb's lettuce), cabbages, savoy, white and red cabbage, chicory, celery, fennel.

(c) (the root of the plant): carrots, beetroot, radishes (black and ordinary), stachys (or Japanese artichoke), celeriac, onions, garlic, kohlrabi, horse-radish, etc.

(d) (the flower of the plant): asparagus, Brussels sprouts.

4. *Leguminous plants:* young green peas, beans, etc.

5. *Cereals:* wheat, oats, maize (Indian corn), rice preferably in the form of flakes or wholemeal flour.

6. *Nuts, almonds, olives:* walnuts, hazelnuts, pine kernels, Brazil nuts, coconuts, sweet almonds. *Olives* cannot be eaten raw because they are too bitter; yet they are valuable food and may be profitably eaten when they have been commercially pickled or pasteurized, if they are put in water to remove the brine. The olive oil is the most valuable part of the olives. Peanuts (ground nuts) are less to be recommended, as according to Haig's researches they help to produce uric acid.

7. *Vegetable spices:* caraway seeds, fennel seeds, capers, chervil, borage, tarragon, chive, parsley, etc.

8. *Milk, milk products and eggs:* sweet and sour cream; condensed sweet or unsweetened milk, which having been heated is not especially good as food, but excellent as a means of binding various components. It also helps people to get accustomed to the taste of raw food.

FOODSTUFFS

9. *Honey:* can be used in the same way as condensed milk, as an addition, as a means of binding components, and to help the taste.

RECIPES OF UNCOOKED DISHES

IV

Recipes of Uncooked Dishes

By intelligent combination many varied dishes may be prepared from amongst the great number of foodstuffs that can be eaten raw. They are remarkable for their purity and pleasant taste. Refined French cooking knows such raw food under the name of hors d'oeuvre. Unfortunately they are, as a rule, prepared with mustard, spices and vinegar, thus inducing people to drink, but lessening their value from the health point of view. In conclusion only a small number of recipes will be added, built on the preceding principles. They are just examples. Any woman, experienced in the art of cooking, will easily be able to find out and prepare new combinations.

A. RAW FRUIT PORRIDGE (Bircher Muesli)

The recipe given is the portion for one person.

1. *Apple Muesli*
    1. *Apples.* Two or three small apples or one large one. Clean them by rubbing with a dry cloth. Do not take away the skin, core or pips.

RECIPES OF UNCOOKED DISHES

2. *Nuts.* Walnuts, hazelnuts, almonds—one tablespoonful.
3. *Rolled Oats.* * A level tablespoonful previously soaked in 3 tablespoonfuls of water for 12 hours.
4. *Lemon Juice.* The juice of half a lemon. †
5. *Top milk (T.T.) and honey or sweet condensed milk* (Nestlé's). One tablespoonful.

Preparation:

First mix condensed milk (or top milk and honey) and juice of lemon with soaked rolled oats. Then grate the apples including the skin, core and pips vigorously into the mixture on a two-way grater (see Illustration 6) and whilst doing so, stir continually. In this way the apple pulp is covered by the mixture and thus prevented from getting brown in contact with the air. It looks white and appetizing. The dish should be prepared immediately before being put on the table. ‡ The grated nuts or almonds (1 tablespoonful) which are sprinkled over the dish increase the protein content and fat.

This dish is served fresh, before anything else, and is not intended as dessert. The fact that it is cold is never harmful as long as the muesli is well chewed and thus sufficiently warmed in the mouth. For those of a nervous disposition it may be warmed, but not above 95°F., as otherwise its nutritive value would be impaired.

This dish is especially suitable as a wholesome break-

---

*A level teaspoonful or dessertspoonful of medium stone-ground oatmeal, previously soaked, is perhaps preferable, as it is not precooked. It is obtainable at health food stores. (C.L.)

†When lemons are difficult to obtain, less juice may be used—from a teaspoonful onwards. (C.L.)

‡If the muesli is taken on a trip or to the office, the best way is at once to fill a bottle up to the brim and make it airtight by fixing the lid with a rubber ring. In this way it can be kept fresh for several hours.

fast and supper for children from the age of two*, for sick people with digestive disorders and for healthy people who wish to remain healthy.

The well-known medical authority, Doctor Ry of Milan, reporting on this dish in the "Corriere della Sera" and enjoying it very much, gave it the beautiful name "la dolce sorpresa" (sweet surprise)! It is becoming widely known in England as "muesli."

The preparation of the dish as given above has proved to be the best after the experience of thirty years. Thus rolled oats are found to be preferable to other cereal products, but on no account should more than a level tablespoonful be used per person. †

The condensed milk is preferable to cream or honey as a means of binding. It does not clot, does not get sour, is perfectly pure and easily obtained. It is produced in a vacuum at a low temperature and still contains to a large extent the vitamins of raw milk.

The juice of lemon is rich in minerals and vitamins. Apples are grown in our part of the world and if picked and stored with care can be kept in good condition for months. They must be used with the skin, and especially also with the core, as the latter contains, besides other valuable constituents, twenty-four times as much iodine as the rest of the apple.

According to the season, and to give a change, the dish can be varied in different ways.

1

Instead of the condensed milk one may use a *tablespoonful of honey.* In order to make the honey suitable for the mixture a pound of honey and three tablespoonfuls of water are warmed in a pan of water,

---

*See Bircher-Benner: *Children's Diet Book.* (Keats Publishing).
†See page 17 footnote.

RECIPES OF UNCOOKED DISHES

and stirred continually until the water and honey are well mixed.

2

Those who do not like sweet things may use a tablespoonful of unsweetened condensed milk instead of the sweetened condensed milk, or *a tablespoonful of cream.*

3

Instead of the rolled oats one may take: a level tablespoonful of wheatflakes, or a tablespoonful of whole wheatmeal, or a tablespoonful of whole rye meal (all of them soaked beforehand in the manner described above).

It may here be noted that oats are usually chosen for the combination, because of the widespread belief in their nutritive value. This belief, derived from notions about the proper feeding of horses, is quite without foundation, since whole wheat and whole rye have an equally great nutritive value. As people have been taught that fruit contains little protein and has therefore no appreciable nutritive value the compounding of this dish of fruit diet is often changed in such a manner that a great deal of oats is used and little fruit. In consequence the dish loses its flavour and its real nutritive value, in short its "raison d'étre."

These dishes were originated on the basis of the new discovery that fresh fruit has a specially high nutritive value and is surprisingly well utilized in the digestive tract, provided it reaches the stomach properly broken up.

It is not the oats but the fresh fruit of this dish that gives the nourishment. And the best supplement to the fresh fruit is the nuts, a very small quantity of which is sufficient.

It is because of the quite special nutritive value of fruit that apples are used with the skin, the core and pips, all finely grated, and with other suitable fruit; and in the case of other suitable fruits also, the *whole* fruit should be in like manner turned to account. The nutritional teaching which has been fully set forth in *Food Science for All* arrives at the conclusion that the true nutritive principle does not reside in a plurality of substances, but rather in something that subsists between the substances—in the harmonious interaction of all the materials united by Nature within a single food. To express the same thing in terms of energy, it resides in the calculated and graded play of rainbow colours inside the food, considered as a total combination of the energies of sunlight.

If we take only *parts* of the natural food for our nourishment, we disturb the proportions of energy on which depend the normal course of life and in the last resort its very continuance. People would do well to study carefully the results of vitamin research; they are a simple confirmation of this teaching.

To what great extent the quantitative proportions of the residue of combustion of ashes can be changed, if instead of eating a whole apple we eat only its pulp, can be seen by the analysis of the apple "ashes" which Dr. J. Konig gives us in his great work on foodstuffs:

Analysis of residue	Total ash of dry substance %	Potash %	Soda %	Lime %	Magnesia %	Oxide of iron %	Phosphoric acid %	Sulphuric acid %	Silicic acid %
Whole fruit of apple	1.44	35.68	26.09	4.08	8.75	1.40	13.59	6.09	4.32
Fruit pulp only	1.75	41.85	—	8.85	5.05	—	9.70	—	—

Everyone can thus see that the whole fruit supplies an exact quantity of soda in relation to an exact quantity of potash; the pulp supplies only potash. The entire fruit supplies iron, sulphuric acid and especially silicic acid, the pulp gives none of these, while many important combinations of phosphorus are lacking in the fruit pulp. These elements nature has put into the skin, the core and the pips of the apple, which are essential to its nutritive value. Everyone knows that iron and phosphorus are important nutritive minerals, but only a few people know that silicic acid is of the greatest significance for the eyes, the skin, the hair, the teeth and the whole connective tissue.

Many so-called educated people laugh at the idea of feeding sick people "with the remains of apples." They would do better to start feeding their children straight away on the raw fruit porridge, using the whole apple, skin, core, pips and all, since already "the axe is laid unto the root of the trees"! The time is coming when we shall be amazed at the people of the past who tried to make their children and invalids strong with masses of protein, extracts of meat, cod liver oil, etc.

Since even nowadays people still inquire about the calorific value of food, it is added here to the first recipe. The weight of each ingredient is given as a basis.

Quantities of weight of one portion:
    Apples 5¼ oz.
    Rolled oats ⅜ oz.
    Nestlé's Milk ⅛ oz.
    Juice of half a lemon ⅜ oz.
    Nuts ⅜ oz.
    Water 1⅜ oz.
    Total weight = 7⅞ oz.

This portion after combustion in the organism supplies calories as follows:

Protein	Fat	Carbohydrates	Total
20.3	74.2	136.0	230.5 Calories

Now take 100 calories of this dish and compare with the same amount of mother's milk:

	Protein Calories	Fat Calories	Carbohydrate Calories
Muesli	8.8%	32.2%	59.0%
Mother's milk	7.4%	43.9%	48.7%

as opposed to

	Protein Calories	Fat Calories	Carbohydrate Calories
Food of the upper classes*	19.2%	29.8%	51.0%
Food of workmen.*	16.7%	16.4%	66.9%

The dream of the physiologist Rubner that a diet might be found for children and adults, the composition of which would be identical with mother's milk, is thus realized in this dish. It has full calorific value and is a food that corresponds with the laws of the human organism. It is equally valuable from the "energizing" point of view.† Its contents of vitamins, of minerals in organic combination and natural flavours, satisfy the most strictly scientific demands and cannot be surpassed by other food.

2. *Blackberry muesli.*

The recipe is the same as for the apple muesli, only instead of the 5¼ oz. of apples, 5¼ oz. of blackberries are used. They are carefully selected, washed in running water and made into a thin pulp, either by putting them through the mincer or by crushing them with a pestle.‡

---

*In Germany.
†See page xiii footnote.
‡Berries can be made into a pulp by crushing with a fork.

RECIPES OF UNCOOKED DISHES

In a similar way one can prepare:

3. *Strawberry muesli.*

4. *Raspberry muesli.*

5. *Currant muesli.*

6. *Gooseberry muesli.*

7. *Bilberry muesli.*

If instead of apples other fruit is used, the required preparation follows naturally.

8. *Cherry muesli.*
The cherries are carefully selected and washed, freed from stones and put through the mincing machine.

9. *Damson muesli.*
The same proceeding as with cherries.

10. *Apricot muesli.*
The same proceeding as with cherries.

11. *Banana muesli.*
The bananas are put through the mincing machine and at once stirred together with the mixture of rolled oats, water, condensed milk and lemon juice. Of course the banana skins are taken off.

Muesli with Dried Fruit

If the season or any other insuperable obstacle makes it impossible to get fresh fruit, it is possible to make this dish with dried fruit. Dried fruit has first to be washed in hot water, then soaked in cold water for twenty-four hours, as described above.

Instead of the 5¼ oz. of apples of the first recipe, take per portion 3½ oz. of dried fruit. Although the fruit has been soaked in water, careful mastication is necessary, so that the digestive organs thoroughly utilize the material. The soaked fruit is put through the mincing machine* and chopped as finely as possible.

Thus one can prepare:

12. *Prune muesli.*

After having been soaked, the prunes are freed of the stone.

13. *Dried apple muesli.*

14. *Dried banana muesli.* †

These fruit dishes are especially suitable for breakfast and supper. If a piece of wholemeal bread‡ is taken with them and a cup of lime blossom tea, hip tea§ or any other harmless tisane with some milk, one is suffi-

---

*Bananas, however, can be crushed easily with a fork.

†Muesli is an all-the-year-round dish, and in normal times is easy enough to make. Food scarcity may necessitate the use of more dried fruit, but this should only be resorted to when no fresh fruit is available. An emergency substitute in early Spring is carrots (3 oz. per person, peeled and grated, then stirred quickly into the ground mixture); these need more sweetening and lemon flavour. Raw rhubarb juice may also be added (2 oz.); it can be made in a juice extractor, or by grating wiped and washed unpeeled rhubarb on a two-way grater into a bowl covered with a piece of butter muslin. Then squeeze muslin and add juice to the ground mixture. (C.L.)

‡An excellent simple recipe, involving no kneading, is given in Doris Grant: *Recipe For Survival* (Keats Publishing). No one who has tasted real bread such as this will want to return to the usual shop-bought stuff. (R.S.)

§See Bircher-Benner: *Children's Diet Book* (Keats Publishing) for directions for making rose-hip tea.

ciently nourished and in a wholesome way; the digestive organs can easily do their work. Those who prefer it can take a cup of coffee free of caffeine with milk.

B. COLD FRUIT DISHES (Macédoine)

These fruit dishes can be used as entrées for tired people, those who come to meals too late or those whose teeth require food that is easily chewed. But they can also be served as dessert instead of stewed fruit, which through cooking has lost much of its freshness, nutritive value and taste. They are also excellent for the sickroom, as they demand but a small effort on the part of weak or feverish patients and their nutritive value is remarkable. A little sugar may be added whenever there is no imperative reason to avoid sugar altogether. Instead of sugar, honey may also be used.

One specimen follows—everybody can easily vary the combinations.

Cold mixed fruit dishes

COMPONENTS

¼ pt. of non-alcoholic apple or grape juice.
1 teaspoonful honey.
1 apple, peeled and cut into fine slices.
1 orange, peeled and cut with a sharp knife into thin slices, diagonally to the axis.
1 banana, similiarly cut into slices.
The kernels of 3 walnuts or 8 hazelnuts.
1 tablespoonful of sweet or sour cream.

Preparation:
The fruit juice, the cream and honey are well mixed

together and stirred, the cut fruit at once added and covered with the liquid. The nuts, either whole or grated, are sprinkled over the mixture. The dish which is now ready should be served at once and eaten quite fresh. This portion is for one or two persons.

This cold fruit dish is also very good when prepared at the beginning of a meal, without cream or nuts. Even the fruit juice can be replaced by water.

These fruit dishes can, of course, be made with all sorts of fruit and berries, such as apricots, plums, grapes, peaches, strawberries, raspberries, currants, melons, pineapples, almonds, pine kernels, in any combination preferred.

C. FRUIT JUICE MIXTURES AND NUT MILK

Fruit juice mixtures and nut milk are of priceless value in certain states of illness, such as fever, children's diseases, the breaking down of digestive and combustive powers, caused either by grave disorders of the stomach and the bowels or by circulation troubles of the heart and blood vessels, liver and kidney diseases, or by old age.

In all these cases these dishes are far superior to a milk diet. They are invaluable against diseases of metabolism, such as gout and obesity. What is aimed at in such cases is the temporary reduction of food to a minimum in order to obtain the combustion of fat, to neutralize the poisoning effects of uric acid and to bring about its excretion. Anyone who understands how to observe such cases will be convinced of the astonishing nutritive power of this food. These nutritive juices are, as it were, the "mother's milk" of those who are seriously ill, the only food they are still able to take. But they are not be considered as mere beverages. The

RECIPES OF UNCOOKED DISHES

patient is not to *drink* them, he is to *eat* them. One small spoonful after another is to be taken and slowly swallowed.

There is very little to be added concerning their preparation, as everything follows naturally from what has already been said. Berries, grapes, peaches, plums, apples and pears, etc., are pressed through the juice extractor (Illustration 3); oranges and lemons with squeezers (Illustrations 1 and 2).

Examples

No. 1.
   6 tablespoonfuls freshly pressed apple juice.
   6 tablespoonfuls freshly pressed orange juice.
   1½ teaspoonfuls freshly pressed lemon juice.
   1 level teaspoonful sweet or sour cream
                     or
   1 level tablespoonful condensed Nestlé's Milk
                     or
   1 level teaspoonful liquefied honey.

These four ingredients are thoroughly mixed by stirring and served at once.

No. 2.
   6 tablespoonfuls freshly pressed cherry juice.
   6 tablespoonfuls freshly pressed strawberry juice.
   1½ teaspoonfuls freshly pressed lemon juice.
   1 level tablespoonful cream or condensed milk or honey.

No. 3.
   6 tablespoonfuls freshly pressed peach juice.
   6 tablespoonfuls freshly pressed raspberry or currant juice.

1½ teaspoonfuls freshly pressed lemon juice.
1 level tablespoonful cream or condensed milk or honey.

No. 4. *Almond Milk.*

Almonds are scalded in boiling water and the skin taken off. Cut off a small shaving of each almond and taste it to see if it is sweet. The bitter almonds are not used for invalids.

Thirty of the sweet almonds thus selected are put into cold water for some hours, then each is carefully dried with a clean cloth and they are pounded in the mortar for 10-15 minutes to a very fine pulp. While continually stirring with the pestle, add a teacupful of cold water, filter the whole through a fine linen cloth which is finally pressed as much as possible. Add, if desired, a tablespoonful of fresh milk or cream, or a pinch of vanilla.

The more finely the almonds are crushed the better the milk will be.*

Nut milk added to the fruit juices is liquid food of the highest value for sick children, grown-up people who are seriously ill, and the aged.

D. RAW VEGETABLES

As has already been mentioned, the cleaning and choice of materials must be done most carefully.

---

*Almond purée, made from blanched almonds, is particularly suitable for small infants and people with delicate digestive organs. (C.L.)

To get a glass of nut milk, take a level tablespoonful of nut butter (N.B. level with a knife and see that no butter is clinging to the underneath of the spoon), and mix in a cup, adding water drop by drop whilst continually stirring until a fairly liquid mixture is obtained. With the addition of more water a milky emulsion is produced so that the beverage, when ready, looks exactly like ordinary milk. One can add some brown sugar, some honey, fruit-juice, fresh milk, cream or a pinch of vanilla, according to taste.

RECIPES OF UNCOOKED DISHES

Raw vegetables are of the highest order amongst foodstuffs. They are superier to cooked food, not only in nutritive value but also from the point of view of taste. Of course they can be added to any meal like any other salad and thus increase the supply of uncooked material. Our health can only gain by this. But for therapeutic purposes too, whole meals can be prepared of only such raw vegetables, muesli, fruit and nuts or of raw vegetables alone (when and how this is to be done is for the doctor to decide). Where it is expedient a diet consisting exclusively of uncooked vegetables or combined with the fruit and nut diet may be arranged for whole days or series of days. The curative effect of such a diet when judiciously used is astonishing and unfortunately too little known.

In order to prepare meals of this kind, the raw vegetables must be combined properly in suitable groups. For the sake of simplicity only a few groups of raw vegetables are here given as examples, and at the same time particular recipes are added. When raw vegetables are only given as an addition to other dishes, one single vegetable is chosen, prepared and served together with the cooked food. If, however, one wants to prepare a meal entirely of uncooked vegetables, or with a combination of the fruit and nut diet, a whole group of raw vegetables is chosen and nicely arranged in a dish. Of course a great many groups can be arranged owing to the variety of vegetables. There is ample scope for the individual taste. Only a few examples are given here. By adding aromatic herbs, onions, leeks, etc., the taste can be very greatly stimulated, while the addition of olive oil and cream prevents it from being overstimulated. Moreover oil and cream increase the calorie value of these dishes in a surprising way. It would hardly be possible to get in another way such a plentiful supply of fat with an equally good result, and this is especially important in the case of diabetes.

There can be no question of adding any salt. For therapeutic purposes salt must be avoided altogether. It is quite unnecessary in the case of raw vegetables, which are rich in nutritive minerals, i.e. have their own salts containing the most valuable properties. When people are not yet used to this superior kind of food, salt may be added at first, but as little as possible.

Fruit and nut diet, raw vegetables, uncooked food! It will probably be thought that I am trying to increase the number of "faddists" of the uncooked food movement and to fight against cooking, the value of which cannot possibly be doubted. Doubtless the "man in the street" with his sound common sense (that is, the man who lives in fear of having to think things out for himself!) would thus turn away from me and not consider my teaching worthy of any consideration whatsoever. But the thoughtful person will protect me against such intentional misinterpretation. He will not forget that I stand for a more correct valuation of nutrition, since a wrong valuation has been taught for a long time and prevails everywhere, a valuation that creates many serious diseases. If there were no over-valuation of cooked food, I should have no occasion to plead for uncooked food.

My purpose is not to support faddists, but to help those who know the real value of uncooked food and make use of it in order to avoid unnecessary chronic ill health.

E. RAW FOOD DISHES (hors d'oeuvres)

The quantities indicated in the following raw food dishes are for one person, but they are merely estimated on an average and can be altered according to circumstances. The selection of vegetables, also, is only given by way of example. The taste of the person for whom the dish is intended should be considered within reasonable limits; though here there are certain qualifications to be made. There are people who like onions, while others do not—but the fact is that onions are an excellent food and an effort should be made to make a small quantity of finely grated onions acceptable even to those who dislike them. Garlic is often avoided because of its persistent smell, but it has an excellent influence on the function of the intestines; it calms down flatulence and bears with it special nutritive values. For all these reasons it should be added to the dishes, but in very small quantities; when this is done the smell is not offensive. Ample uses should be made of radishes and tomatoes. People generally like the radishes, and according to popular belief they are instrumental in dissolving gall stones and kidney stones. Should this prove to be a fact, then there is no reason why they should not also prevent the formation of stones. In my opinion, not only radishes, but all raw vegetables and fruit too, possess such medicinal power. Tomatoes occupy today a very high place in scientific estimation. They are noted for their abundance of all vitamins. All the medical objections raised against tomatoes, especially the one respecting their oxalic acid, have proved to be groundless. It is, however, a good thing not to be one-sided in the choice of vegetables, but rather to range as wide as possible. Increasingly it is dawning upon us that each of these plants, roots, leaves and herbs, edible in the raw state, possesses special nutritive and curative powers, and, one might add, protective value.

Therefore cabbages, fennel, carrots, beetroot,

celeriac, kohlrabi, cucumber, dandelion leaves, leeks, aromatic herbs and pot herbs should also be used. I should like to put in a word even for horse-radish, in spite of the sharp taste. When used in small quantities it adds to the tastiness of the dish, and helps to accustom people to food to which no cooking salt has been added.

These additions to the vegetables can be arranged in little heaps round the edge of the dish, so that the real gourmet can select them according to his taste. Or one can make a selection of finely chopped aromatic herbs worthy of a Brillat-Savarin—and mix them with grated onions, garlic, leeks, purslane, etc., plenty of olive oil and some lemon juice, perhaps also some mayonnaise. A very tasty salad dressing is thus obtained, which is poured over the raw vegetables. A little honey added to this salad dressing is very pleasant.

Some people object to all this work of grating raw vegetables and preparing them with olive oil and lemon juice. They have either been affected by the teaching of false prophets, or else they are people who have retained excellent teeth. There was a man in my Sanatorium so stuffed with queer ideas that he brought to the luncheon table the whole head of cabbage, declaring this to be the real food for men. To the great amusement of the other guests he began to nibble the cabbage. A few days later he changed from a rodent into a carnivore, went to an hotel and devoured animal prey! People with excellent teeth may eat raw food in any way they please, provided they take care to chew well. They are unfortunately the great exception. Out of a thousand people, nine hundred and ninety-nine have bad teeth, in spite of toothbrush and toothpaste, because they have been feeding on cooked food all their life. The nine hundred and ninety-nine need grated

RECIPES OF UNCOOKED DISHES

raw food, carefully prepared.

A few examples of raw food dishes are given.

Note: The quantities given in the first four examples are intended for *one* person.

1. Raw Food Dish

Carrots, White Cabbage and Lettuce

1¾ ozs. carrots are finely grated (Illustration 4).
1½ ozs. white cabbage are finely cut or sliced with the cucumber slicer.

A plate with a weight upon it is pressed on the cabbage to soften it and thus left for some hours.

Both vegetables are now put side by side on a small plate.

Salad Dressing:

2 tablespoonfuls olive oil*
2 teaspoonfuls fresh lemon juice
1 teaspoonful cream
1 teaspoon-tip honey
1 teaspoonful finely grated onions.
Some finely cut chives and parsley.
1 teaspoon-tip of grated garlic.
A small quantity of fresh aromatic herbs. In winter dried herbs may be used. †

---

*Instead of olive oil, mayonnaise can be substituted (a heaped-up teaspoonful). Recipe: To the yolk of an egg add 2 tablespoonfuls of olive oil drop by drop, stirring continually until a thick emulsion is formed. Add a teaspoonful of lemon juice and stir.

†Such herbs as thyme, marjoram, tarragon, borage, mint, etc.

Stir all these ingredients well, and pour the salad dressing over the two vegetables.*

> 2 ozs. lettuce. Pour 2 tablespoons olive oil and ½ teaspoon lemon juice over them and mix well.

Arrange this salad side by side with the two vegetables—or serve in a separate dish.

2. Raw Food Dish

Cauliflower, Tomatoes and Endive

1¾ ozs. raw cauliflower, finely grated.
3 ozs. tomatoes, finely sliced.
Arrange the two vegetables tastefully side by side on a dish. Pour salad dressing (see recipe 1 above) over them.
1¾ ozs. endive salad, finely cut. Prepare like lettuce salad and use it to garnish the two other raw vegetables.

3. Raw Food Dish

Celeriac, Red Cabbage, Corn Salad and Lettuce

1¾ ozs. finely grated celeriac.
1 oz. red cabbage, finely cut and pressed like white cabbage (see recipe 1 on page 33).
Arrange the two vegetables on a plate.
¾ oz. corn salad, prepared like lettuce, is put round the red cabbage by way of garnishing. Pour salad dressing over it (see above).
1¾ ozs. lettuce. Prepare as in former recipes.

---

*It is left to the individual taste to make these dishes as palatable as possible. The mere addition of some onion sometimes improves the taste. Experience alone can teach.

RECIPES OF UNCOOKED DISHES

4. Raw Food Dish

Kohlrabi, Tomatoes with Mayonnaise and Fennel

1¾ ozs. finely grated kohlrabi.

1¾ ozs. fennel, finely cut or sliced and softened for some hours under pressure like white cabbage (see page 33).

Arrange the two vegetables side by side on a plate—pour salad dressing (see page 33) over them.

2½-3 ozs. tomatoes are halved and filled with 1½ tablespoons mayonnaise.

Salad Dressing:

The composition of the salad dressing can be varied according to taste. Olive oil and lemon juice alone can be used and the small grated additions used as garnishing or sprinkled over the raw vegetables. Cream or another oil can be used instead of olive oil, but olive oil is the purest and the most beneficial.

Green Salad Dressing:

3-4 tablespoons finely chopped herbs—chervil, tarragon, cress and tender spinach leaves—are pressed through the mincer. The juice thus obtained is mixed with mayonnaise previously prepared.

Garnishing:

Watercress, parsley, capers, gherkins, shallots and olives can all be used for garnishing.

5. Raw Food Dish

Celeriac, radishes, beetroots, carrots, cucumber, tomatoes, spinach, leeks, cabbage, onions, garlic and all sorts of aromatic herbs.

This dish is intended for 2-4 people and is suitable also for a small family, say, as the main raw dish, supplemented by cooked food.

    3½ ozs. celeriac
    5¼ ozs. radishes
    3½ ozs. beetroot
    3½ ozs. carrots

Each of these is grated separately.

    5¼ ozs. cucumber } both cut into slices (not too fine), the cucumber must not be pressed nor salted.
    7 ozs. tomatoes

    2¾ ozs. spinach leaves
    1 small leek } cut into fine strips.
    ½ small cabbage

Dilute 3½ ozs. mayonnaise with 1 tablespoon lemon juice, 3 tablespoons olive oil and 1 tablespoon liquefied honey. Dress each vegetable, except the tomatoes, with the mixture. Drop some lemon juice on the tomato slices and plenty of olive oil as well.

Arrange the vegetables thus prepared on a flat round dish so as to produce a harmonious colour scheme.

Finely chopped onions, or small whole onions, chopped herbs, strips of green pepper pod or capsicum or lettuce may be used as garnishing. Pour a few drops of lemon juice and olive oil over the garnishing too. Green peas are put on small yellow lettuce leaves in the centre of the dish. The garnishing vegetables are arranged in narrow strips between and round the other vegetables.

RECIPES OF UNCOOKED DISHES

F. RAW VEGETABLE JUICES

To give an idea of the quantities of vegetables required for the juices:

100 grams (3½ ozs.) of juice are obtained from the following amounts of vegetables:
- 200 gr. (7 oz.) of lettuce
- 200 gr. (7 oz.) of spinach
- 160 gr. (5½ oz.) of tomatoes
- 260 gr. (9 oz.) of radishes
- 440 gr. (15½ oz.) of carrots
- 300 gr. (10½ oz.) of beetroot
- 400 gr. (14 oz.) of onions

It is best to use the mincer (Illustration 3) to obtain the juice. For the mixed juices (see below) it is advisable to have the vegetables mixed before pressing them on the screw-press.

The vegetable juices are generally insipid to the taste. They must therefore be made palatable by a suitable addition of aromatic herbs finely pounded. Vegetable juices can also be mixed and aromatic herbs added.

Examples of vegetable juices:*

1. 6 tablespoonfuls radish juice, 1 tablespoon cream, parsley and rosemary.

---

*These are merely suggestions for suitable combinations of juices—everyone will find out the right combinations for himself. The important things are (i) to include as many vegetables as possible, (ii) to see that the three parts of the plant (root, leaf, fruit) are all represented. Though the juice of green leaves is the most valuable of the ingredients, care must be taken that the mixture is not made bitter by too much of this. A good base of carrots and tomatoes allows for a larger quantity of green leaf juice without making the whole mixture unpalatable. (C. L.)

2. 6 tablespoonfuls beetroot juice, 1 tablespoon lemon juice, parsley and pimpernel.

3. 6 tablespoonfuls carrot juice, 1 tablespoon cream, 1 tablespoon lemon juice, tarragon and basil.

4. 6 tablespoonfuls spinach juice, 1 tablespoon sweet condensed milk, mint and marjoram.

5. 6 tablespoonfuls spinach juice, 1 tablespoon cream or olive oil, ½ tablespoon lemon juice, mint and marjoram.

6. 6 tablespoonfuls tomato juice, ½ - 1 tablespoon lemon juice, 1 tablespoon cream-basil.

Mixed Juices

7. 6 tablespoonfuls tomato juice, ½ teaspoon lemon juice, 1 tablespoon olive oil, tarragon, rosemary and basil.

8. Three tablespoonfuls beetroot juice, three tablespoonfuls lettuce juice, 1 dessertspoonful onion juice, 1 tablespoon cream or olive oil, mint and marjoram.

9. Three tablespoonfuls spinach juice, three tablespoonfuls carrot juice, 1 tablespoon olive oil, ½ tablespoon lemon juice, chives and parsley.

10. Three tablespoonfuls radish juice, 3 tablespoonfuls carrot juice, 1 tablespoon olive oil, ½ tablespoon lemon juice, rosemary, chives and parsley.

A glass of nut milk (see page 28 footnote) must always

be added to these juices when no other food is taken.

G. EXCLUSIVE RAW FOOD DAY

Days or weeks of *exclusively* raw food diet are only ordered in case of special chronic diseases, which, however, are very widespread.

Sometimes one day of the week is set apart as a *raw food day* in the same way that a day of fasting has been the religious tradition for centuries. The food taken on such days is as follows:

Breakfast: Muesli with some nuts. Choice of fresh fruit, rose-hip tea, mint tea, or some similar beverage.

Lunch: Choice of fruit or macédoine of fruit, nuts. A dish of raw vegetables. Non-alcoholic apple or grape juice.

Supper: Muesli with nuts. Choice of fruit. Tisane.

In certain cases a Liquid Raw Food Day is prescribed.

Breakfast: 7-14 ozs.* mixed fruit juice. 7 ozs. nut milk.†

Lunch: 7 ozs. mixed fruit juice. 7 ozs. nut milk. 7 ozs. vegetable juice. Apple or grape juice.

Supper: 7-14 ozs. mixed fruit juice. 7 ozs. nut milk.

These juices are to be eaten with a small spoon or sucked through a straw. They must be well insalivated.

---

*1 oz. may be taken as equivalent to 2 tablespoonfuls of liquid or 1 tablespoonful of purée. (C.L.)
†Made from 1 level tablespoonful of nut milk diluted (see page 28 footnote) (R.S.)

H. MENUS FOR RAW FOOD MEALS

A raw food lunch consists of the following courses:

1. Choice of the best fruit—or macédoine of fruit; walnuts or hazelnuts or sweet almonds or pine kernels. (If the teeth are not good, the almonds must be pounded.)

2. A dish of raw vegetables, well assorted and varied.

SPRING (March, April, May)

1. Apples, bananas, walnuts, slices of red radishes on finely cut lettuce, fennel with mayonnaise, garnished with cress—lettuce salad.

2. Oranges, nuts, finely chopped spinach, beetroot, radish mixed with some horse-radish—lettuce salad.

3. Macédoine of fruit, pine kernels, cauliflower, slices of tomatoes, corn salad—lettuce salad.

4. Oranges, almonds, hazelnuts, finely cut tender sugar-peas (pois mange-tout), red cabbage, celeriac with parsley—lettuce salad.

5. Apples, bananas, nuts, tomatoes filled with green salad dressing, savoy cabbage, radish—lettuce salad.

6. Oranges, nuts, carrots, dandelion, red radishes—lettuce salad.

7. Bananas (or strawberries), pine kernels, kohlrabi, cubes of tomatoes, watercress—lettuce salad.

RECIPES OF UNCOOKED DISHES

SUMMER (June, July, August)

1. Strawberries, almonds, hazelnuts, slices of tomatoes topped with grated cauliflower and fine herbs (basil, dill, parsley), finely cut sorrel—lettuce salad.

2. Cherries, nuts, lettuce, beetroot, stems of celery with lemon dressing—lettuce salad.

3. Raspberries, and currants, nuts, carrots and onion mixed (finely grated), young green peas with mayonnaise, garnished with finely cut spinach—lettuce salad.

4. Peaches, apricots, cherries, almonds, hazelnuts, spinach-beet surrounded by a wreath of radishes and garnished with tomato cubes—lettuce salad.

5. Bilberries with cream, celery, red cabbage, garnished with borage and capsicum—lettuce salad.

6. Plums, pears, nuts, cucumber, tender Indian corn dressed with mayonnaise, spinach—lettuce salad.

7. Peaches, plums, apples, nuts, kohlrabi, tender finely cut beans, tomatoes, parsley—lettuce salad.

AUTUMN (September, October, November)

1. Pears, grapes, nuts, grated pumpkin and radish (mixed), spinach-beet, beetroot—lettuce salad.

2. Peaches, plums, nuts, aubergines (eggplant), leeks, carrots, parsley—lettuce salad.

3. Apples, plums, nuts, white cabbage, tomatoes stuffed with chopped onions, pimpernel and dill, cucumber—lettuce salad.

4. Pears, plums, almonds, hazelnuts, chicory, cauliflower, beetroot—lettuce salad.

5. Peaches, grapes, nuts, salsify, red cabbage, corn salad—lettuce salad.

6. Apples, pears, nuts, celeriac, garnished with finely cut spinach-beet, tomatoes, chives—lettuce salad.

7. Bananas, peaches, pine kernels, cucumber, carrots, purslane—lettuce salad.

WINTER (December, January, February)

1. Tangerines, apples, nuts, fennel, spinach, cubes of tomatoes—endive salad.

2. Grapes, pears, nuts, brussels sprouts, carrots mixed with horse-radish, cress—lettuce salad.

3. Tangerines, bananas, almonds, hazelnuts, Japanese artichokes, tomatoes, leeks—lettuce salad.

4. Apples, grapes, nuts, chopped spinach, turnips, stems of celery—lettuce salad.

5. Tangerines, almonds, hazelnuts, tomatoes stuffed with horse-radish, celery and watercress, garnished with lettuce leaves—endive salad.

RECIPES OF UNCOOKED DISHES

6. Pears, apples, nuts, lettuce, cucumber, cauliflower, garnished with parsley—lettuce salad.

7. Oranges, nuts, winter cabbage, Japanese artichokes, carrots, cress—lettuce salad.

These few hints for the preparation of uncooked food can serve various purposes. First they may induce the mistress of the house to enrich the ordinary meal with those dishes that would greatly further the welfare of the family. Secondly they are the best instruction for those who are the victims of a wrong diet; they enable the patients to carry out their dietetic treatment under the doctors control. Then, too, doctors can use them for their patients; they may be a welcome relief from their usually complicated prescriptions.

Qui bene nutrit, bene curat — good food means good cure!

V

Examples of Diet Days

*As prescribed in Dr. Bircher-Benner's Sanatorium
Arrangements and calculations by*
MAX EDWIN BIRCHER, M.D.

Anyone who has seriously tried to adopt—or persuade others to adopt—the new diet, has met with sundry difficulties not easily overcome. First of all he has to get acquainted with the new principles of cooking,* thanks to which it is possible to prevent the deterioration of foodstuffs attending the customary way of cooking. Then the sense of taste has to be developed and refined so that palatable dishes can be produced with a minimum of salt. The cook has to learn the flavour of food anew, thereby discovering qualities hitherto unnoticed. Aromatic herbs, fallen into oblivion, have once more made their entry into the kitchen garden.

The preparation of raw food meets with little understanding. In the popular mind, raw food means "eating grass." Even amongst medical men and hospital nurses

*See concluding paragraph of Preface, page xv.

EXAMPLES OF DIET DAYS

such comical notions are current. They have often prevented a start being made in the new direction.

The first pages of this booklet tell us in what lavish way nature offers us foodstuffs which may be eaten unchanged except by ordinary cleaning. Unfortunately many of us are so "denatured" that it takes a long time to make us appreciate the value of such food.

The most difficult thing of all is to apply the fine theories to practical life, to fix upon the food that contains, not only the necessary calories, but also all other indispensable nutritive elements in correct correlation, and which at the same time abounds in variety.

Stricter diets are herewith given for the sick and the best way to carry out a diet of exclusively raw food is indicated. There follows a menu for fruit-fasting, an even stricter variety of the raw food diet, and a milder variation of raw diet with a supplementary dish of cooked food.

1. NORMAL DAY

The normal diet herewith described is one in which the cooked vegetable food and the raw edible food about counterbalance each other. With this normal diet, too, the raw food is an integral part, and the cooked food retains its importance in so far as it has not deteriorated or lost its nutritive value through too long cooking or processes of preservation.

Our normal diet is made up of two simple meals, one in the morning and one at night, and a third, more plentiful, in the middle of the day. Note that the muesli is served twice a day and that the mid-day meal always begins with raw fruit.

RAW FRUITS AND VEGETABLES BOOK

NORMAL FOOD DAYS

Simple Menus (suitable for household meals):

Breakfast:	Muesli	7-10½ ozs.
	Milk or rose-hip tea	1 cup
	Nuts*	¾ oz.
	Wholemeal bread	2-5 ozs.
	Butter	½ oz.

Lunch:	Raw fruit and nuts	3½-7 ozs.
	Soup or all sorts of vegetables	7-10½ ozs.
	Potatoes or farinaceous dish	7 ozs.
	Raw vegetable dish and lettuce salad	3½-7 ozs.

(Eggs are only used as a means of binding other foods together, and then very sparingly.)

Supper:	Muesli	7-10½ ozs.
	Lime-blossom tea or rose-hip tea	1 cup
	Wholemeal bread	2-5 ozs.
	Butter	½ oz.
	Perhaps the remains of the mid-day meal	

More Elaborate Menus

(For sanatoria, clinics, etc.):

Breakfast:	Muesli	3½-8½ ozs.
	Choice of fresh raw fruit	3½ ozs.

* Not peanuts.

EXAMPLES OF DIET DAYS

Various nuts*	¾ oz.
Wholemeal bread	2-3½ ozs.
Butter	½ oz.
Milk,† rose-hip tea or lime-blossom tea, nut milk, occasionally sour milk or yoghurt	1 cup

Lunch:

Choice of fresh ripe fruit	3½-7 ozs.
Vegetable soup or oatmeal soup, etc. (See *Health-Giving Dishes*. There is no soup on the day on which there is a sweet.)	1 plate
Vegetables of all kinds (steamed or cooked in such a way as to make use of the water in which they have been boiled).	3½-7 ozs.
Potatoes	1¾-3½ ozs.
Farinaceous dish in moderation‡	1¾-3½ ozs.
Lettuce salad	1¾ ozs.
Dish of raw vegetables	1¾ ozs.
Sweets (fruit tarts, stewed fruit, puddings) in moderation	1¾-3½ ozs.
Wholemeal bread	1¾ ozs.

(Eggs are only used as a means of binding when preparing the dishes. They must be used sparingly.)

*Not peanuts.
†Milk only when it is scrupulously pure and preferably unboiled.
‡The use of wholemeal products is preferable. The best way to turn cereals to good account is to grind them by means of a grinding-mill shortly before making use of them.

Supper: Muesli — 3½-8½ ozs.
Choice of fresh raw fruit — 3½ ozs.
Various nuts* — ¾ oz.
Wholemeal bread — 2-3½ ozs.
Butter — ½ oz.
Rose-hip tea (etc.) — 1 cup

Perhaps an additional, but not necessary, dish of lettuce salad, raw vegetables and, by way of exception, some cooked vegetables.

Examples of a Normal Food Day with Calculation of Calories

BREAKFAST	Quantities in ozs.	Protein	Fat	Carbohydr.	Total
		Cal.	Cal.	Cal.	Cal.
Muesli	7	16.5	60.6	111.0	188.1
Walnuts	¾	9.8	98.6	8.8	117.2
Wholemeal bread	3½	26.4	6.3	211.6	244.3
Butter	½	0.3	76.2	0.2	76.7
Oranges	3½	2.9	—	53.6	56.5
1 lump of sugar	¼	—	—	20.0	20.0
TOTAL	15½	55.9	241.7	405.2	702.8

LUNCH	Quantities in ozs.	Protein	Fat	Carbohydr.	Total
		Cal.	Cal.	Cal.	Cal.
Oranges	3½	2.9	—	53.6	56.5
Walnuts	¾	9.8	98.6	8.8	117.2
Wholemeal bread	3½	26.4	6.3	211.6	244.3
Rice with tomatoes	7	17.6	56.3	111.1	185.0
Spinach	5	9.4	30.4	19.5	59.3
Lettuce salad	1¾	1.5	82.0	4.0	87.5
Japanese artichoke salad	2½	4.0	127.0	50.3	181.3
TOTAL	24	71.6	400.6	458.9	931.1

* Not peanuts.

EXAMPLES OF DIET DAYS

SUPPER	Quantities in ozs.	Protein	Fat	Carbohydr.	Total
The same as breakfast	15½	Cal. 55.9	Cal. 241.7	Cal. 405.2	Cal. 702.8
All three meals together		183.4	884.0	1269.3	2336.7

2. TRANSITIONAL DAY

If, besides having to provide the organism with full-value nutritive material, the new diet has also to be instrumental in overcoming illness of long standing and assist in the curative process, raw food must be given the primary place in the menu: a great choice of the best fruit will be provided and at the mid-day meal a carefully prepared and thought-out dish of raw vegetables. All cooked food is of secondary importance. This is the diet we call *transitional*.

TRANSITIONAL MENUS

a. normal form **b. liquid or purée**

Breakfast:

a. normal form		b. liquid or purée
Muesli	5¼-7 ozs.	Muesli with especially finely grated fruit; perhaps with cream and fine (instead of medium) oatmeal, 3½-7 ozs.
Nuts of all kinds*	¾-1 oz.	
Fruit	3½-7 ozs.	
Wholemeal bread	1 oz.	
Butter	¼ oz.	Nut milk 5¼ ozs.
Rose-hip tea	1 cup	Fruit juice or hip tea 1 cup
		Some bread and butter (on condition that it is well chewed).

*Not peanuts.

Lunch:

Fruit	3½-5¼ ozs.	Fruit juice	3½-7 ozs.*
Vegetable soup	1 plate		
Lettuce salad, raw vegetables	½ portion	Lettuce salad finely chopped	1¾ ozs.
Cooked vegetables	½ portion		

Potatoes, farinaceous dish, small quantity

Raw vegetables pounded in the mortar or strained (cucumber, tomatoes, etc.) 3½ ozs.

Vegetable juice (spinach, carrots, etc.) with some cream, olive oil and lemon juice 3½ ozs.*

Potato soup‡ with vegetable broth and strained cooked vegetables 1 plate

Nut milk ca. 7 ozs.*

Perhaps apple juice ca. 7 ozs.*

Supper:

Muesli	5¼-7 ozs.		
Nuts of all kinds†	¾-1 oz.		
Fruit	3½-7 ozs.		
Wholemeal bread	¾-1 oz.		
Butter	¼ oz.		

Muesli with especially finely grated fruit; perhaps with cream and fine (instead of medium) oatmeal 3½-7 ozs.

Nut milk 5¼ ozs.*

Fruit juice or hip tea 1 cup

Some bread and butter (on condition that it is well chewed)

---

*See page 28 footnote.
†Not peanuts.
‡Recipe for potato soup: Fry chopped onions in butter, add vegetables cut into small bits (leeks, celeriac, carrots, cauliflower, savoy, etc.) and fry all together for some minutes. Sprinkle with flour, smooth with water and boil up again. Boil soup for one hour. Then add well-cleaned, unpeeled raw potatoes; boil up again until the potatoes are tender. Strain soup and season with salt, nutmeg and cream.

EXAMPLES OF DIET DAYS

Example of a Transitional Day with Calculation of Calories

Breakfast	Quantities in ozs.	Protein	Fat	Carbohydr.	Total
		Cal.	Cal.	Cal.	Cal.
Muesli	7	16.5	60.6	111.0	118.1
Nuts	¾	9.8	98.6	8.8	117.2
Oranges	3½	2.9	—	53.6	56.5
Wholemeal bread	3½	26.4	6.3	211.6	244.3
Butter	½	0.3	76.2	0.2	76.7
Rose-hip tea with 1 lump of sugar	¼	—	—	20.0	20.0
Total	15½	55.9	241.7	405.2	702.8

Lunch	Quantities in ozs.	Protein	Fat	Carbohydr.	Total
		Cal.	Cal.	Cal.	Cal.
Nuts	¾	9.8	98.6	8.8	117.2
Oranges	3½	2.9	—	53.6	56.5
Lettuce salad ...	1¾	1.5	82.0	4.0	87.5
Raw food dish (celeriac)	2	2.8	155.5	12.4	170.7
Cooked vegetable (spinach)	3½	6.3	20.3	13.0	39.6
Potatoes	1¾	4.3	0.5	42.0	46.8
Total	13¼	27.6	356.9	133.8	518.3

Supper	Quantities in ozs.	Protein	Fat	Carbohydr.	Total
		Cal.	Cal.	Cal.	Cal.
The same as breakfast	15½	55.9	241.7	405.2	702.8
All three meals together		139.4	840.3	944.2	1923.9

3. RAW FOOD WITH A SUPPLEMENTARY DISH

Somewhat stricter is the diet consisting of raw food with certain supplementary dishes given to make the régime more acceptable to the patient, especially when it is cold.

RAW FOOD DAYS

a. with certain supplementary dishes	b. liquid or purée with certain supplementary dishes

Breakfast:

Muesli	5¼ ozs.	Muesli with especially finely grated fruit; perhaps with cream and fine (instead of medium) oatmeal	3½-7 ozs.
Nuts of all kinds*	¾ ozs.		
Fruit	3½-7 ozs.		
Rose-hip tea	1 cup		
		Nut milk†	5¼ ozs.
		Fruit juice or hip tea	1 cup

Lunch:

Fruit or macédoine of fruit	5¼-7 ozs.	Fruit juice	ca. 3½-7 ozs.
Lettuce salad	1¾-3½ ozs.	Lettuce salad, finely chopped	ca. 1¾ ozs.
Raw food dish	3½-5¼ ozs.	Raw vegetables pounded in the mortar or strained (cucumber, tomatoes, etc.)	ca. 3½ ozs.
Nuts of all kinds			
Potatoes, ‡ vegetable broth and steamed vegetables			

---

*Not peanuts.
†See page 28 footnote.
‡Preferably potatoes with caraway seeds. Recipe: Take fairly small potatoes (without taking off their skins), wash them and halve them mid-ways; sprinkle cut surface with a mixture of caraway seeds (or if these are not liked, chopped herbs) and a very little salt (celery salt); lay them, cut surface downwards on a buttered tin, brush them over with melted butter or margarine. Bake about 45 minutes in hot oven.

EXAMPLES OF DIET DAYS

Perhaps 1 glass unfermented apple or grape juice	Vegetable juice (spinach, carrots, etc.) with some cream, olive oil and lemon juice 3½ ozs.*
	Potato soup with vegetable broth‡ and strained cooked vegetables.
	Nut milk ca. 7 ozs.*
	Perhaps apple juice ca. 7 ozs.*

Supper:

Muesli	5¼-8¾ ozs.	Muesli	3½-7 ozs.
Nuts of all kinds†	¾-1 oz.	Nut milk	ca. 7 ozs.*
Fruit	3½-7 ozs.	Fruit juice	ca. 7 ozs.*
Perhaps rose-hip tea	1 cup	Perhaps rose-hip tea	1 cup

4. STRICT RAW FOOD DAYS

By "raw food" we mean a diet composed of uncooked fruit of all sorts, berries, also nuts, hazelnuts or almonds, the fruit of raw vegetables such as tomatoes, cucumbers, zucchetti (squash) and the leaves and roots of raw vegetables, finely grated.

People unaccustomed to raw food should only have raw food for a period, say for a few days, or a few weeks or some months, *according to medical prescription*, depending on the illness to be cured.

Such periods of a diet consisting exclusively of raw food, which is rich in alkalis and vitamins, have a tremendous curative effect.

---

*See page 28 footnote.
†Not peanuts.
‡Vegetable stock: Clean, wash and cut various vegetables (leeks, celeriac, carrots, cabbage, cauliflower); chop onions, fry them in butter, add vegetables and 2-4 quarts of water and boil for an hour. Cleaned scraps of raw potatoes (without their shoots) and bits of other vegetables can also be used. If vegetable stock is wanted for cooking vegetables in and has to be done in a hurry some Marmite and Vecon dissolved in boiling water gives a valuable substitute.

With such a diet the supply of calories is intentionally kept low, for the requirements of the organism are considerably smaller with raw food than with a meat diet and cooked food. It is thus possible to relieve the metabolism, the organs and the circulation and to liberate the chemical combustive powers of the whole system for their internal cleansing processes.

We know by experience that a serious illness or a doctor's profound conviction or the patient's unusual discernment is needed to carry out a strict raw-food period. The more care is bestowed upon the preparation of raw food, the more the dishes are varied—the sooner will misgivings be dispelled, longing for this or that dish disappear, despondency and dejection vanish. In many cases a great sense of relief is experienced after only a few days and this makes the patient of his own freewill see to it that the raw food period is carried through properly.

STRICT RAW FOOD DAYS

a. normal form   b. liquid or purée

Breakfast:

Muesli*	5¼-7 ozs.	Muesli* with especially finely grated fruit; perhaps with cream and fine (instead of medium) oatmeal 3½-7 ozs.
Nuts of all kinds†	¾-1 oz.	
Fruit	3½-7 ozs.	
Rose-hip tea	1 cup	
		Nut milk 5¼ ozs.
		Fruit juice or hip tea 1 cup

*The quantities given are approximate. Only the patient's natural feeling—undeteriorated by stimulants or bad habits—can decide. In cases where a strictly economic diet is aimed at, the feeling or hunger can be lessened by increased chewing and insalivation and very slow eating.
†Not peanuts.

EXAMPLES OF DIET DAYS

Lunch:

Fruit or macédoine of
fruit   5¼-8¾ ozs.
Lettuce salad   1¾-3½ ozs.
Raw food dish   3½-5¼ ozs.
Nuts of all kinds*   ca. ¾ ozs.
Perhaps 1 glass of apple juice
(or other non-alcoholic wine)

Fruit juice   3½-7 ozs. †
Lettuce salad (fine–chopped)
                     1¾ ozs.
Raw vegetables pounded in the mortar or strained (cucumbers, tomatoes, etc.)
                     3½ ozs.
Vegetable juice (spinach, carrots, etc.) with some cream, olive oil and lemon juice
Nut milk   ca. 7 ozs. ‡
Perhaps apple juice ca. 7 ozs. ‡

Example of a Raw Food Day with Calculation of Calories

Breakfast	Quantities in ozs.	Protein Cal.	Fat Cal.	Carbohydr. Cal.	Total Cal.
Muesli	8½	20.2	74.2	136.0	230.4
Nuts	¾	9.8	98.6	8.8	117.2
Tangerines	3½	2.9	—	53.6	56.5
Apples	3	1.2	—	44.8	46.0
Rose-hip tea with 1 lump of sugar	¼	—	—	20.0	20.0
TOTAL	16	34.1	172.8	263.2	470.1

*Not peanuts.
†See page 28 footnote.

Lunch	Quantities in ozs.	Protein	Fat	Carbohydr.	Total
		Cal.	Cal.	Cal.	Cal.
Oranges	3½	2.9	—	53.6	56.5
Bananas	3½	4.5	—	88.0	92.5
Apples	3	1.2	—	44.8	46.0
Walnuts	¾	9.8	98.6	8.8	117.2
Celery salad, prepared	2	2.8	155.5	12.4	170.7
Other salad, prepared	1¾	4.5	166.0	10.2	180.7
Lettuce salad	1¾	1.5	82.0	4.0	87.5
TOTAL	16¼	27.2	502.1	221.8	751.1

Supper	Quantities in ozs.	Protein	Fat	Carbohydr.	Total
The same as breakfast	Cal. 16	Cal. 34.1	Cal. 172.8	Cal. 263.2	Cal. 470.1
All three meals together		95.4	847.7	748.2	1691.3

5. FRUIT FASTING DAYS

Such days are inserted in place of complete fasting. They have the same effect as complete fasting while at the same time avoiding incalculable consequences. Complete fasting means feeding the body on its own material, which leads to autointoxication and deficiency of alkalis. The small fruit meals, because of their first-rate nutritive qualities, have a protective power.

There are special diseases that must be treated with a diet consisting entirely of fruit juices.

EXAMPLES OF DIET DAYS

FRUIT FASTING

a. normal form   b. liquid

Breakfast:

Various fruit	ca. 3½ ozs.	1 glass fruit juice
Nuts (not peanuts)	ca. ½ oz.	1 glass nut milk (without addition of milk or cream)

Lunch:

Various fruit or macédoine of fruit	ca. 5¼ ozs.	1 glass fruit juice 1 glass nut milk
Nuts, almonds	¾ oz.	

Supper:

Various fruit	ca. 3½ ozs.	1 glass fruit juice
Nuts, hazelnuts	ca. ½ oz.	1 glass nut milk

Transitional days and normal food days can be carried out on one's own responsibility without any risk, provided the directions given herewith are followed.

Other diets which entail a reduction of calories should not be adopted without the advice of a practitioner versed in nutrition. It is incumbent upon him to observe and recognize the often far-reaching nutritive effects, to gauge the true proportion of things and to inspire the patient with confidence.

NOTES

NOTES

NOTES